How Emily and Eli Became Friends

Written By: Elsie Guerrero

Illustrated By: Jerome Vernell Jr.

ELSIE PUBLISHING CO.

WWW.ELSIEGUERRERO.COM

I would like to dedicate this book to the children I worked with who are on the spectrum. You are the inspiration to this story.

Definition of Autism:

a condition or disorder that begins in childhood and that causes problems in forming relationships and in communicating with other people

Eli was a charming boy who loved Math and playing football. He went to Chrisen Elementary School and was in the third grade. Eli had lots of friends and loved going to school.

Eli was a very smart, curious, and happy boy.

Emily was a beautiful girl with big brown eyes. She loved to dance, play with play dough, and run around the neighborhood. She also liked specific foods, such as, chips with ketchup and eggs with mayo.

What made Emily unique was that she had autism.

Emily had a tutor for five years who came to her house in the afternoons and helped her with daily life skills, such as brushing
teeth, washing hands, and eating with a spoon.

She also taught Emily fine motor skills, labeling body parts, personal information, and imitation.

After mastering the program, Emily no longer needed a tutor. She was able to live, play and feel like any other kid.

Emily's mother told Emily that she will be starting a new school at Chrisen Elementary School.

Instead of being excited to start a new school, Emily was scared. Emily did not like meeting new people.

The next day, Emily's mother walked Emily to her new school. Emily was so scared that she walked behind her mother covering her face with her mother's purse.

Emily did not like change.

Emily entered the classroom and was frightened by her classmates that she immediately ran out the room.

Her mother found her on the playground and told her that everything will be okay.

Emily was in the same classroom as Eli, who sat across from her. He looked at her desk and noticed that she had pictures and a token board on her desk.

Eli found that strange.

During recess, Eli saw that Emily was running around the playground, screaming, and laughing all by herself.

Eli found that strange.

At lunchtime, Emily was eating
a bowl of chips with ketchup and
drinking pink milk. Eli had never seen
a person eat chips with ketchup.

Eli found her lunch strange.

Eli went home and told his mother all about the new student, Emily. Eli told his mother that she ran out the classroom, screamed and laughed by herself at recess, and had a strange lunch.

Eli's mother told him that Emily has autism.

Eli did not know what autism was. His mother explained "Autism happens in the brain. It slows down Emily's brain and makes it hard for her to talk and play like other kids. She might do things that you would find silly or weird, but it does not make her different from you and me."

Eli found the topic about autism very interesting.

Eli was a curious boy, so he asked his mother if autism goes away.

His mother responded that with treatment, children with autism can live a life just like him.

Eli grasped and was amazed.

The next day, Eli saw Emily running around the playground and decided to join hands with Emily for a game of Ring Around The Rosie.

Emily was so happy in her own little world that she did not notice Eli was beside her. So, Eli just ran and laughed with her.

At lunch time, Eli sat next to Emily and asked her many questions because he was so curious to learn more about autism.

Eli asked ten questions at one time, which became overwhelming for Emily.

Eli paused for a second and asked one question, "what is your favorite color?"

Emily answered, "pink."

In class, Eli was surprised at how good Emily was at Math. Eli loved Math, especially when he gets to count money.

Eli told Emily, "When I grow up, I want to work at a bank! What do you want to do?"

Emily responded, "I don't know".
Eli said, "You are good at Math, maybe you can work with me."

Emily smiled.

From then on, Emily and Eli became best friends.

Emily and Eli would play together during recess. Emily loved running and Eli loved running with her.

Emily would laugh unexpectedly and Eli would join her. Eli learned a lot from Emily. He learned that autism does not make a person strange, but unique.

THE AUTHOR:
Elsie Guerrero

Elsie Guerrero first started working with children with autism in 2011. After working with her clients for six months, she began to develop a passion and desire to represent children with disabilities. Guerrero began to incorporate her passion into her studies and wrote many research papers on special education and disability issues. Her career goal is to become an advocate and a Special Education lawyer. In the meantime, she plans to spread awareness and embrace the beauty of people with disabilities through children's books.

THE ILLUSTRATOR:
Jerome Vernell Jr.

Since a child, born and raised in Baton Rouge, Louisiana, drawing was always his passion.

Now, he is a professional Graphic Designer and Illustrator creating everything from logos to children's books. He is also a loving Husband and proud Father of a 3 year old son.

He loves comic books, movies, and spending quality time with his family.

www.vernell.art

www.ingramcontent.com/pod-product-compliance
Lightning Source LLC
Chambersburg PA
CBHW062012090426

42811CB00005B/830